ED EMBERLEY'S HALLOWEEN DRAWING BOOK

Little Brown and Company   Boston • New York • London

The material in this book was originally published
as part of *Ed Emberley's Big Orange Drawing Book*

ISBN O-316-23481-8

Library of Congress Catalog Card Number 95-77929

10 9 8 7

Printed in Hong Kong

IF YOU CAN DRAW THESE SIMPLE SHAPES

(△ ○ □ D · I L ∧ C)

THERE'S A GOOD CHANCE THAT YOU WILL BE ABLE TO DRAW AT LEAST MOST OF THE THINGS IN THIS BOOK.

STEP-BY-STEP INSTRUCTIONS SHOW YOU HOW.

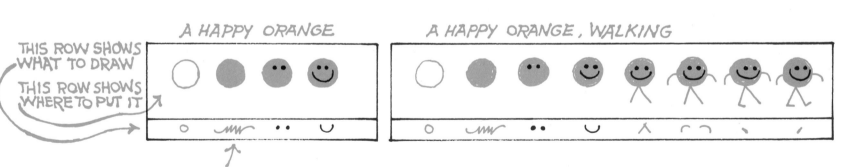

A HAPPY ORANGE

A HAPPY ORANGE, WALKING

THIS ROW SHOWS WHAT TO DRAW

THIS ROW SHOWS WHERE TO PUT IT

THIS SIGN MEANS "FILL IN".

HALLOWEEN SILHOUETTES

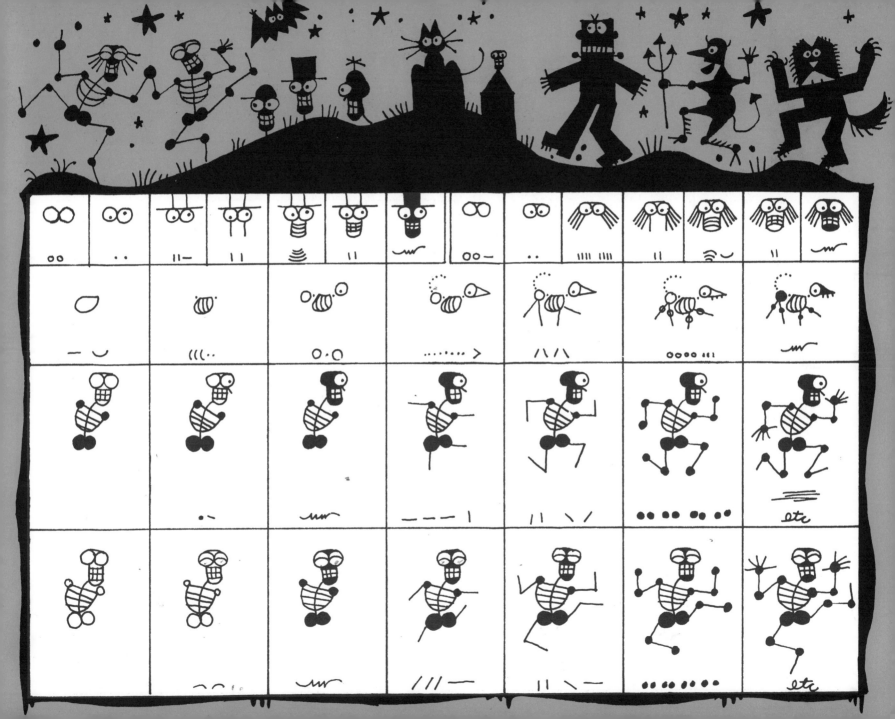

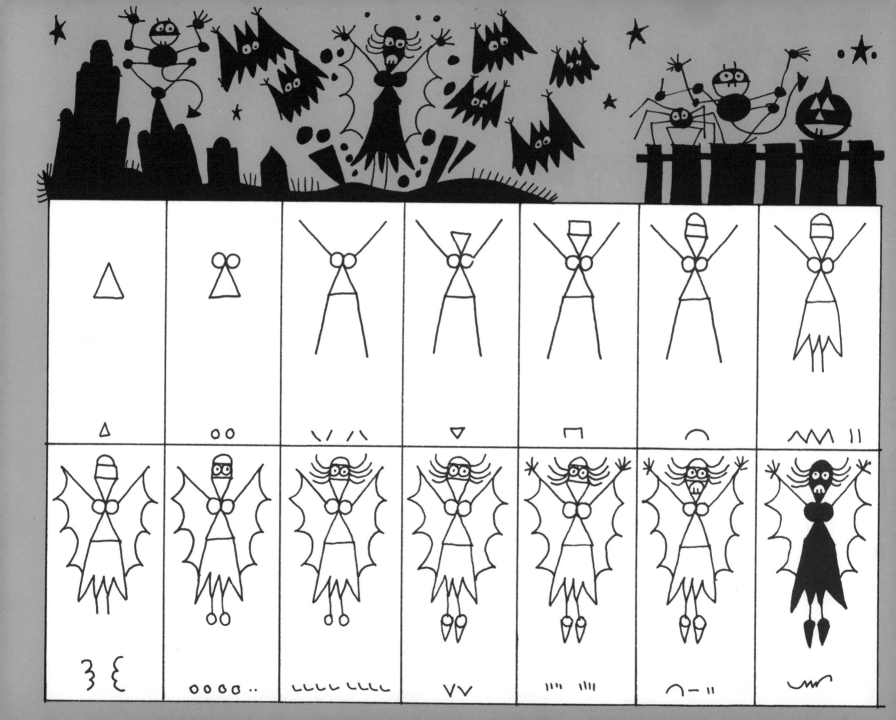

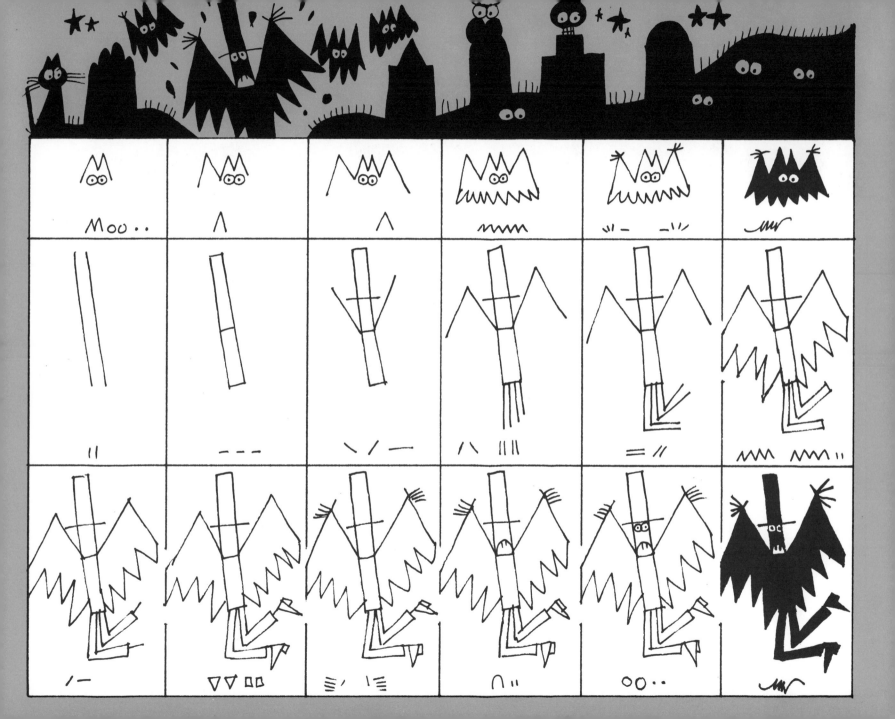

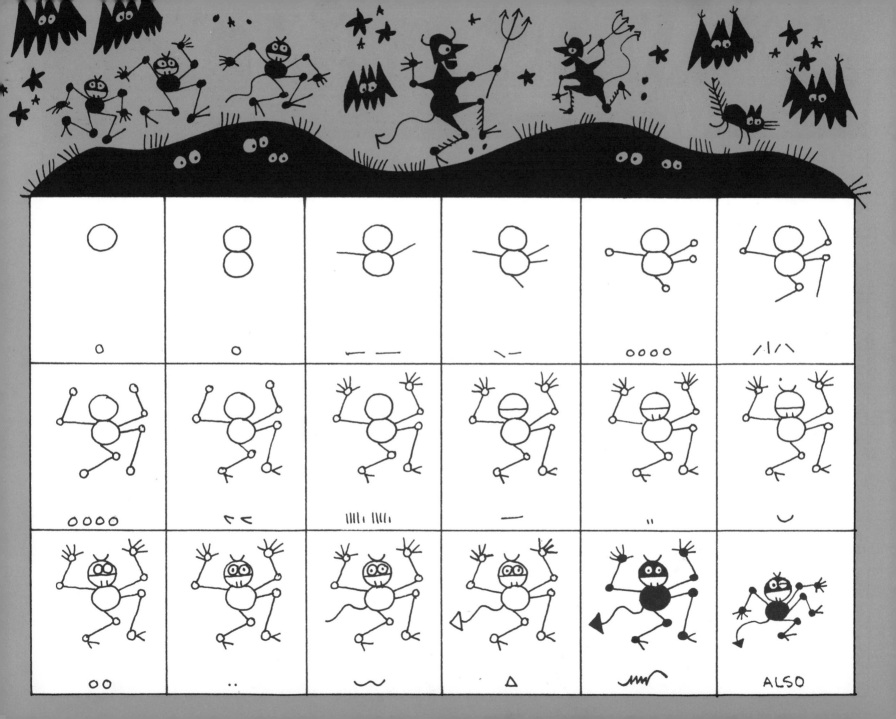

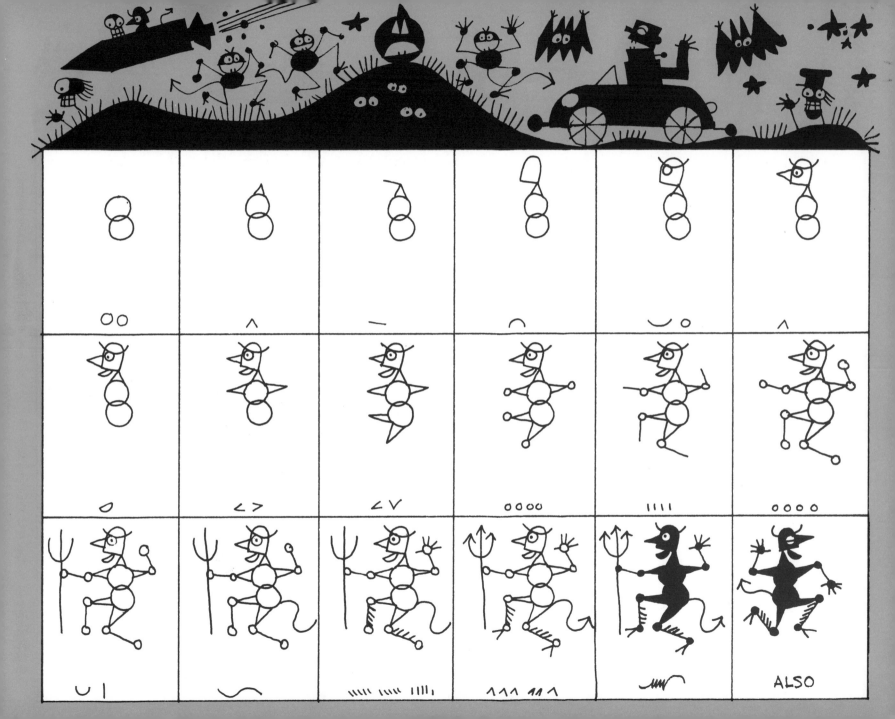

ALSO

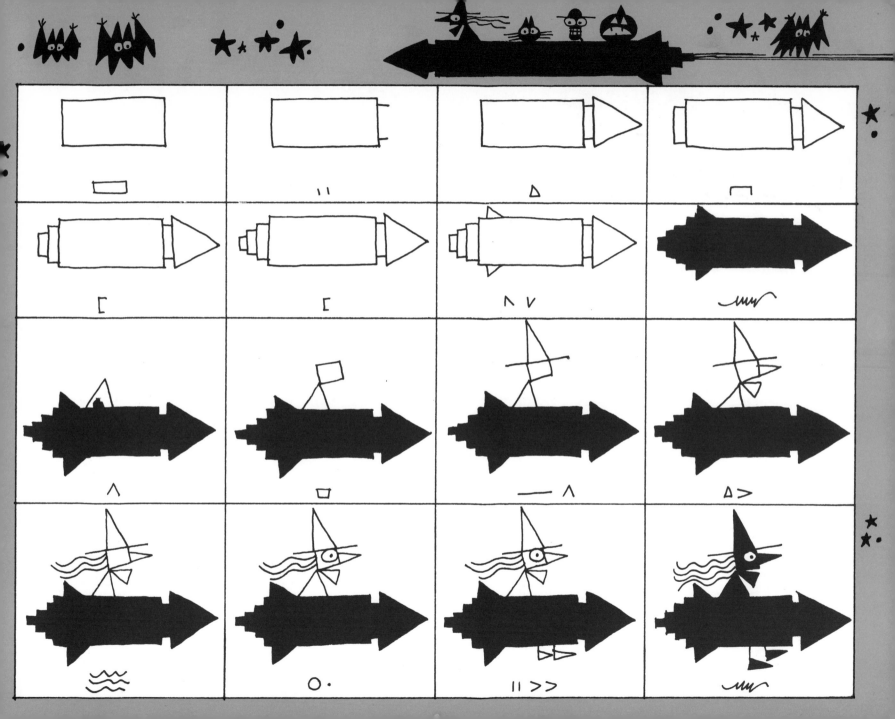

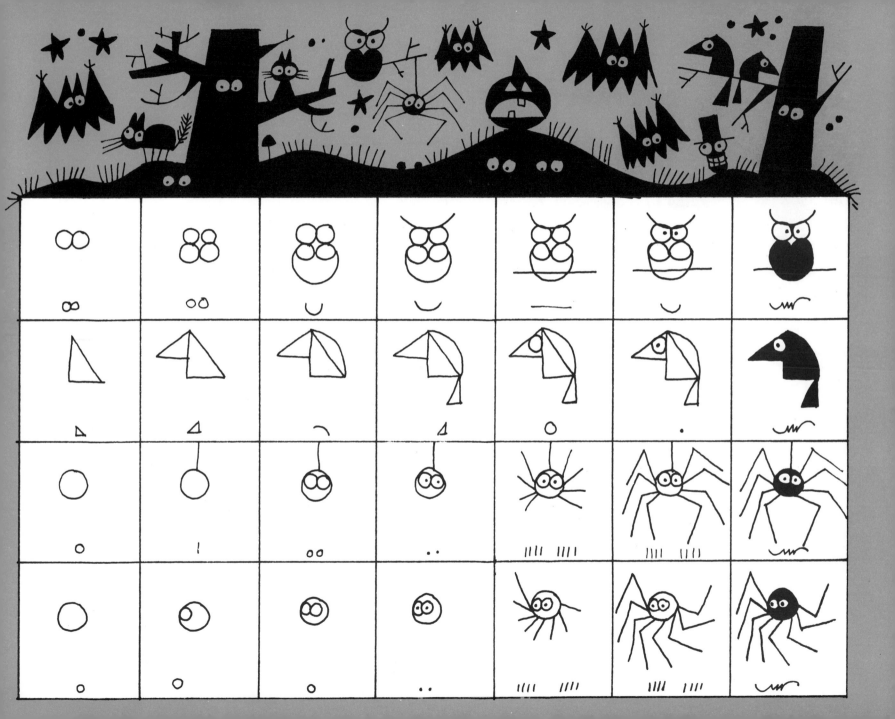

SPOOKY HOUSE

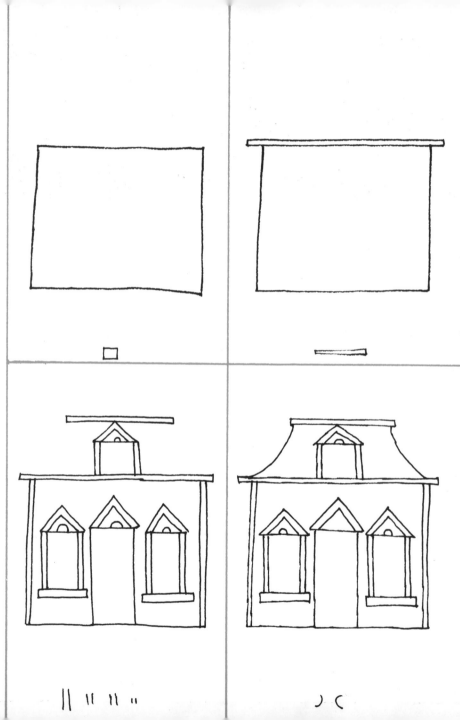

VU etc.

nnnn

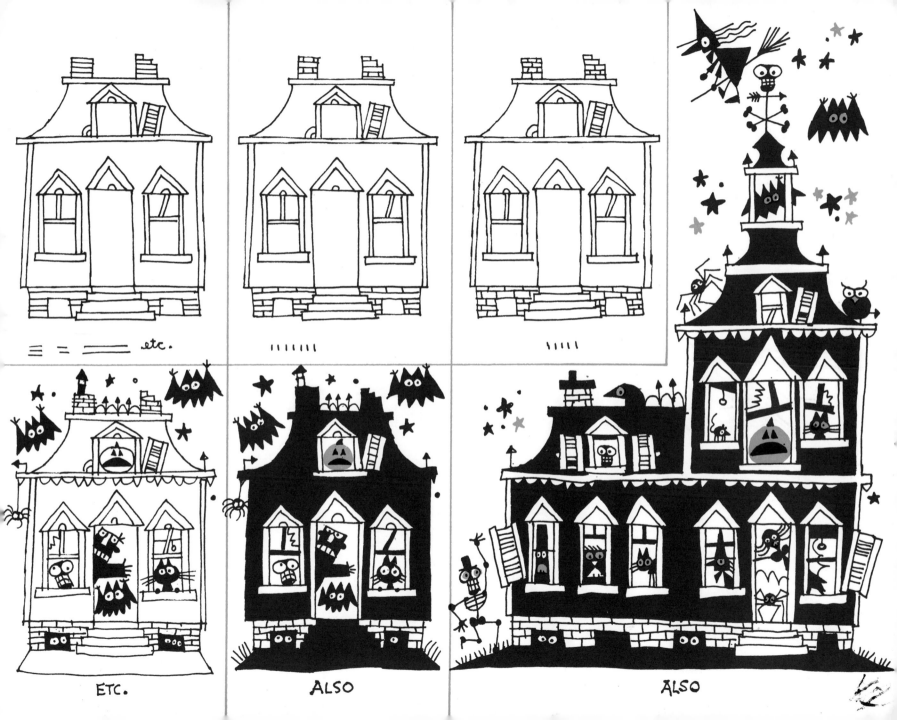

etc.

ETC.

ALSO

ALSO

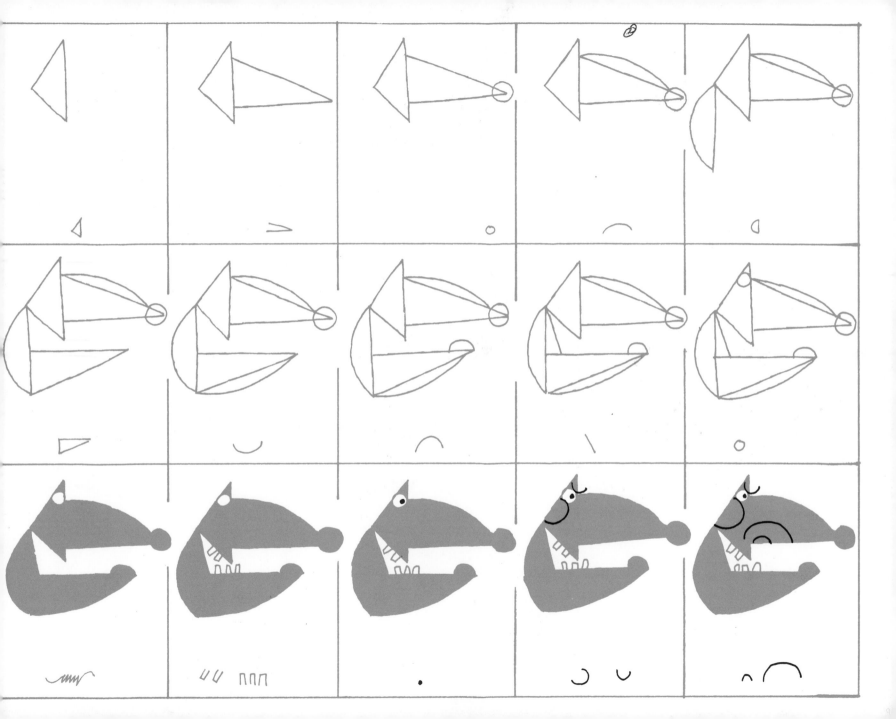

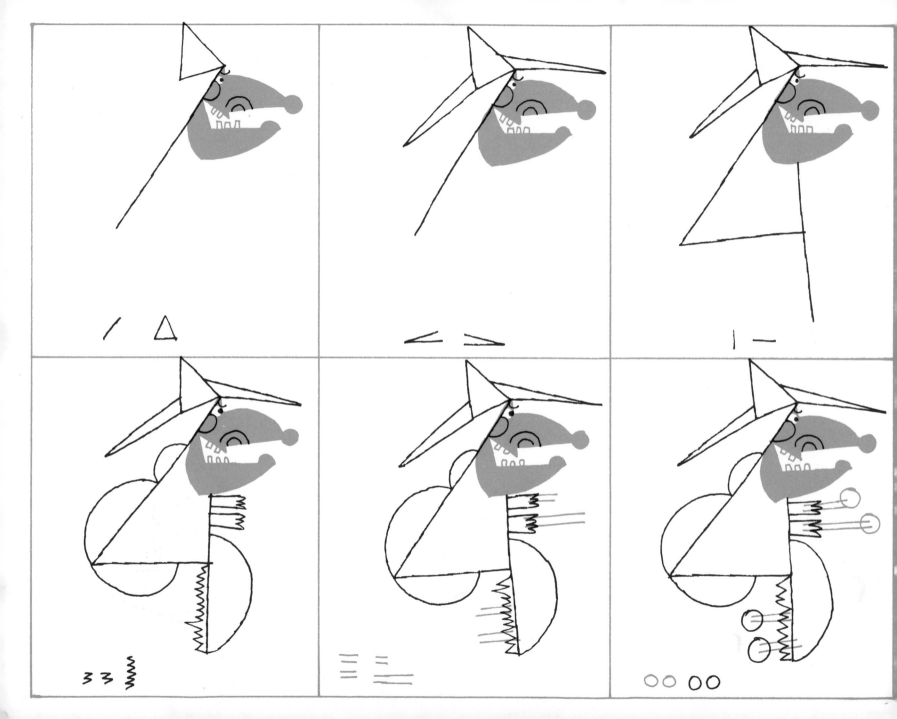

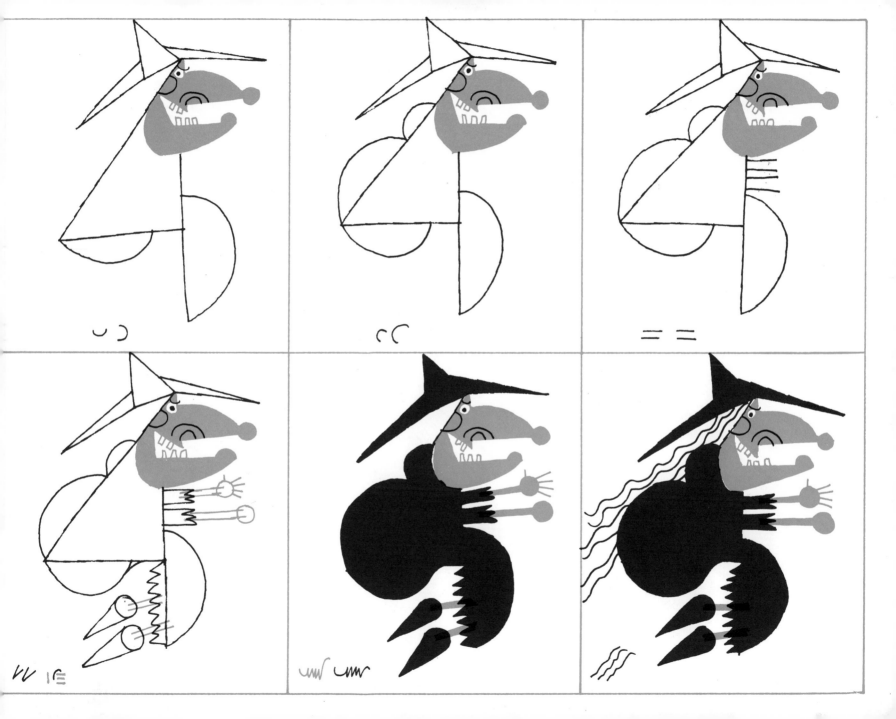

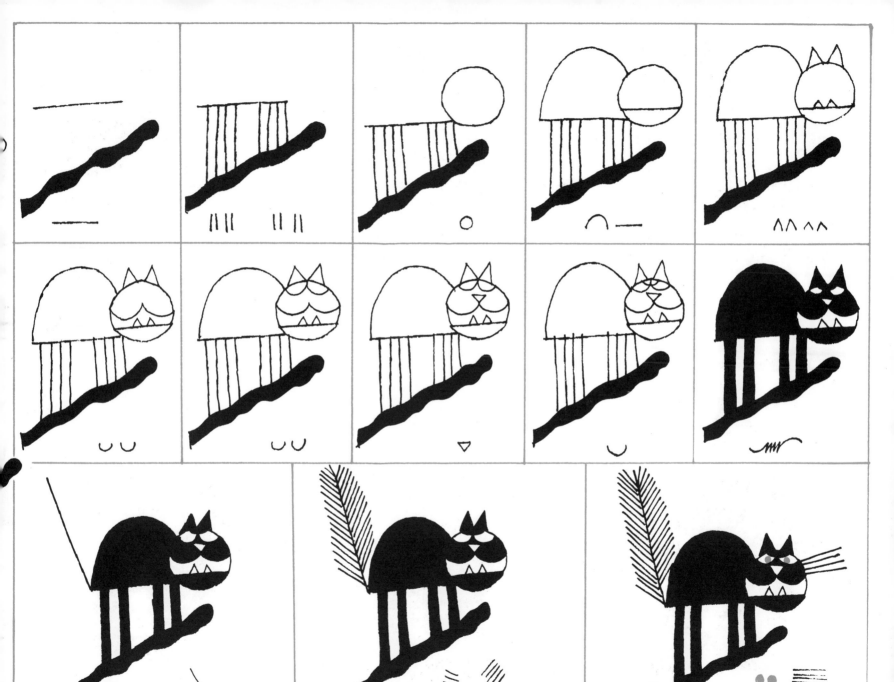

You will find more good Halloween stuff
in these other Ed Emberley Drawing Books: